Celebrating the Anniversary of

_____

Date: _____ Time: _____

Location: _____

_____

Guest Name

Thoughts & Messages
for the Happy Couple

Guest Name

Thoughts & Messages
for the Happy Couple

Guest Name

_____

Thoughts & Messages
for the Happy Couple

Guest Name

_____

Thoughts & Messages
for the Happy Couple

_____

_____

_____

_____

_____

_____

Guest Name

*Thoughts & Messages
for the Happy Couple*

Guest Name

_____

Thoughts & Messages
for the Happy Couple

_____

_____

_____

_____

_____

_____

Guest Name

Thoughts & Messages
for the Happy Couple

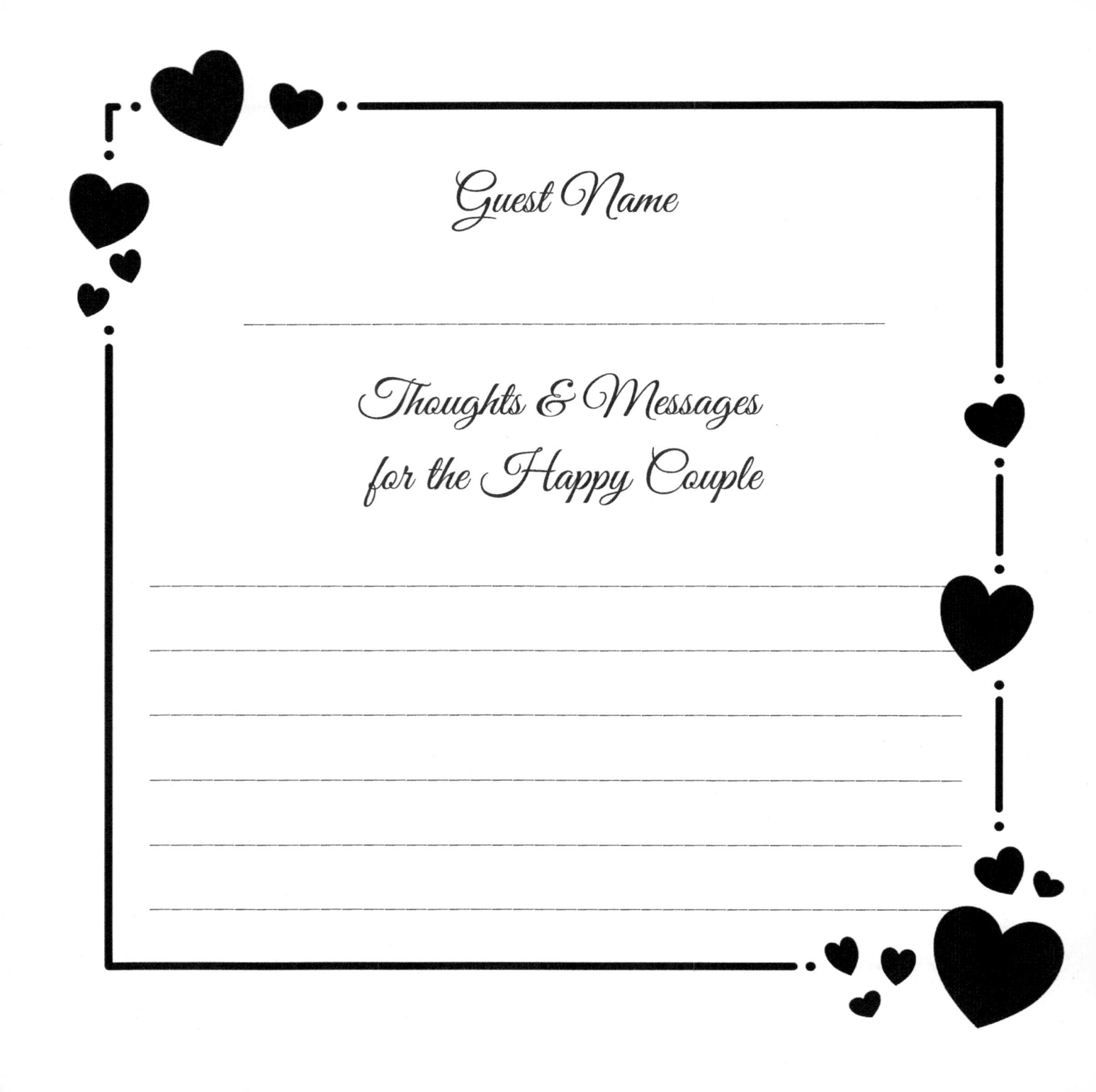

Guest Name

_____

Thoughts & Messages
for the Happy Couple

_____
_____
_____
_____
_____
_____

Guest Name

Thoughts & Messages
for the Happy Couple

Guest Name

Thoughts & Messages
for the Happy Couple

Guest Name

Thoughts & Messages
for the Happy Couple

Guest Name

Thoughts & Messages
for the Happy Couple

Guest Name

_____

Thoughts & Messages
for the Happy Couple

Guest Name

*Thoughts & Messages
for the Happy Couple*

Guest Name

_____

Thoughts & Messages
for the Happy Couple

_____

_____

_____

_____

_____

_____

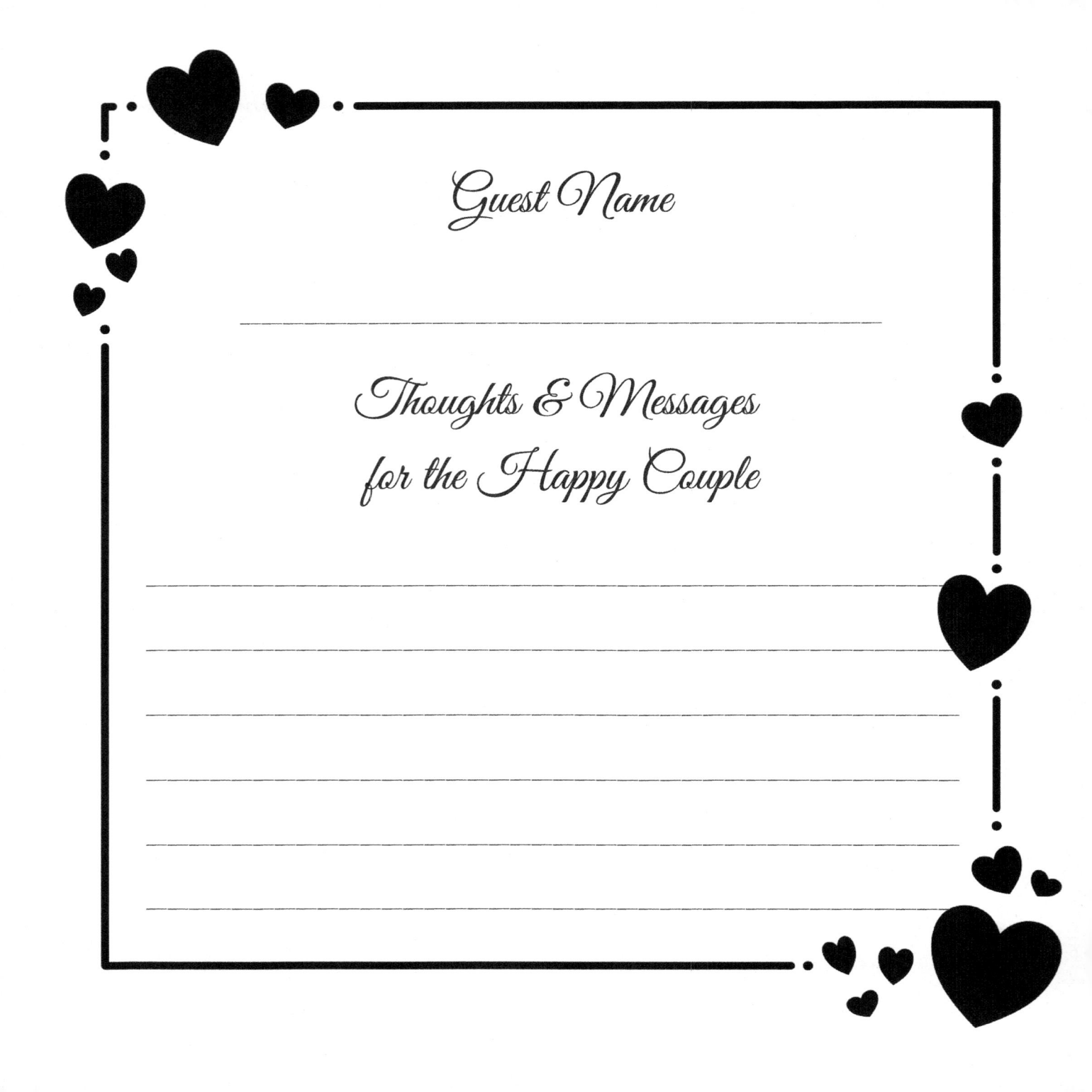

Guest Name

_Thoughts & Messages
for the Happy Couple_

Guest Name

Thoughts & Messages
for the Happy Couple

Guest Name

Thoughts & Messages
for the Happy Couple

Guest Name

Thoughts & Messages
for the Happy Couple

Guest Name

_____

*Thoughts & Messages
for the Happy Couple*

Guest Name

Thoughts & Messages
for the Happy Couple

Guest Name

Thoughts & Messages
for the Happy Couple

Guest Name

_____

Thoughts & Messages

for the Happy Couple

Guest Name

Thoughts & Messages
for the Happy Couple

Guest Name

_____

Thoughts & Messages
for the Happy Couple

Guest Name

Thoughts & Messages
for the Happy Couple

Guest Name

*Thoughts & Messages
for the Happy Couple*

Guest Name

Thoughts & Messages
for the Happy Couple

Guest Name

Thoughts & Messages
for the Happy Couple

Guest Name

Thoughts & Messages
for the Happy Couple

Guest Name

_Thoughts & Messages
for the Happy Couple_

Guest Name

Thoughts & Messages
for the Happy Couple

Guest Name

_____

Thoughts & Messages
for the Happy Couple

Guest Name

Thoughts & Messages
for the Happy Couple

Guest Name

Thoughts & Messages
for the Happy Couple

Guest Name

Thoughts & Messages
for the Happy Couple

Guest Name

*Thoughts & Messages
for the Happy Couple*

Guest Name

Thoughts & Messages
for the Happy Couple

Guest Name

Thoughts & Messages

for the Happy Couple

Guest Name

*Thoughts & Messages
for the Happy Couple*

Guest Name

*Thoughts & Messages
for the Happy Couple*

Guest Name

Thoughts & Messages
for the Happy Couple

Guest Name

Thoughts & Messages
for the Happy Couple

Guest Name

_Thoughts & Messages
for the Happy Couple_

Guest Name

Thoughts & Messages
for the Happy Couple

Guest Name

Thoughts & Messages
for the Happy Couple

Guest Name

Thoughts & Messages
for the Happy Couple

Guest Name

_____

Thoughts & Messages
for the Happy Couple

_____

_____

_____

_____

_____

_____

Guest Name

_____

Thoughts & Messages
for the Happy Couple

Guest Name

_Thoughts & Messages
for the Happy Couple_

Guest Name

_____

Thoughts & Messages
for the Happy Couple

_____

_____

_____

_____

_____

_____

Guest Name

Thoughts & Messages
for the Happy Couple

Guest Name

Thoughts & Messages
for the Happy Couple

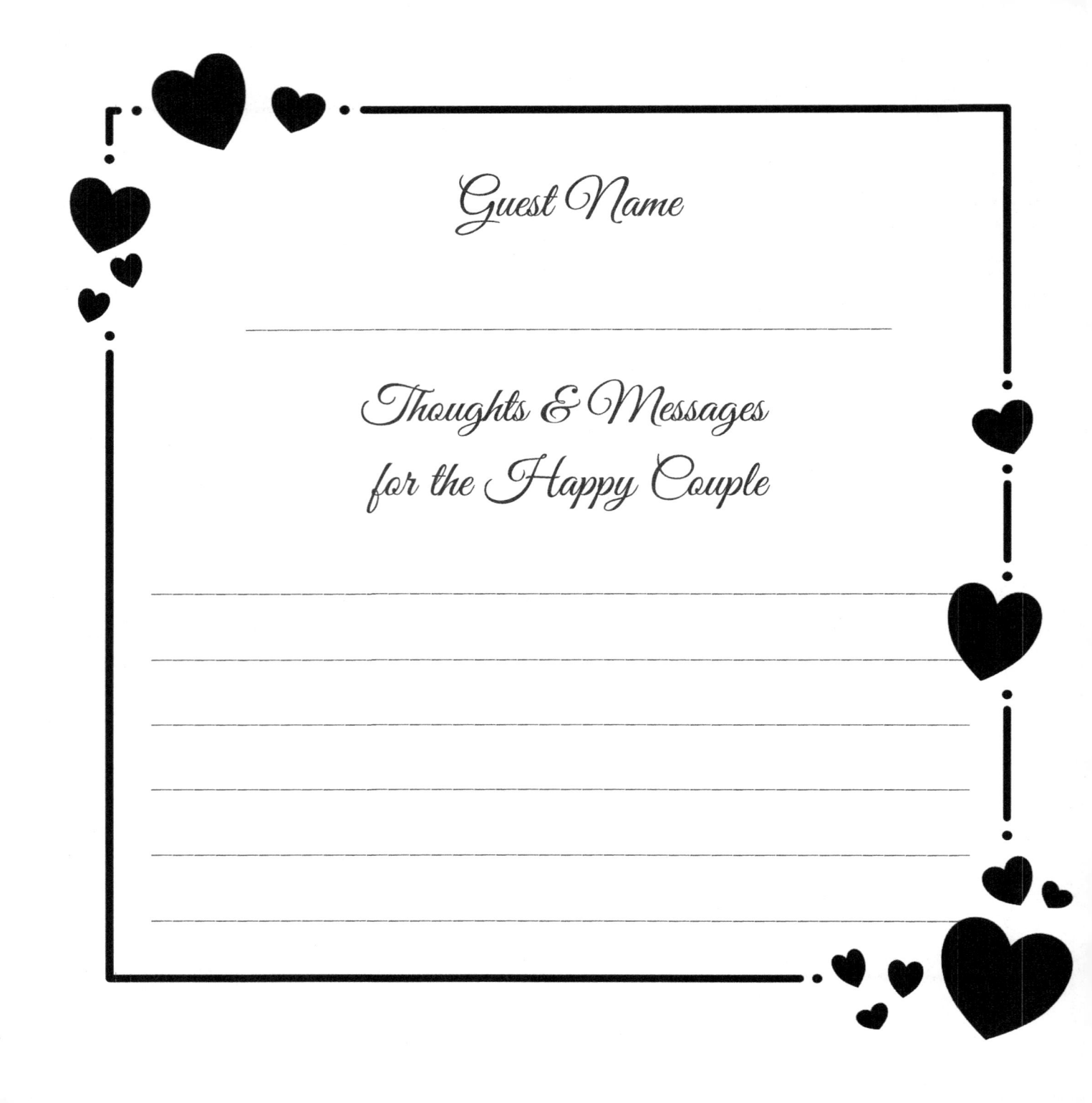

Guest Name

Thoughts & Messages
for the Happy Couple

Guest Name

Thoughts & Messages
for the Happy Couple

Guest Name

Thoughts & Messages
for the Happy Couple

Guest Name

*Thoughts & Messages
for the Happy Couple*

Guest Name

_Thoughts & Messages
for the Happy Couple_

Guest Name

Thoughts & Messages
for the Happy Couple

Guest Name

Thoughts & Messages
for the Happy Couple

Guest Name

_____

Thoughts & Messages
for the Happy Couple

_____

_____

_____

_____

_____

_____

Guest Name

Thoughts & Messages
for the Happy Couple

Guest Name

Thoughts & Messages

for the Happy Couple

Guest Name

Thoughts & Messages
for the Happy Couple

Guest Name

*Thoughts & Messages
for the Happy Couple*

Guest Name

_____

Thoughts & Messages
for the Happy Couple

_____

_____

_____

_____

_____

_____

Guest Name

_____

Thoughts & Messages
for the Happy Couple

Guest Name

Thoughts & Messages
for the Happy Couple

Guest Name

*Thoughts & Messages
for the Happy Couple*

Guest Name

Thoughts & Messages
for the Happy Couple

Guest Name

Thoughts & Messages
for the Happy Couple

Guest Name

*Thoughts & Messages
for the Happy Couple*

Guest Name

*Thoughts & Messages
for the Happy Couple*

Guest Name

*Thoughts & Messages
for the Happy Couple*

Guest Name

Thoughts & Messages
for the Happy Couple

Guest Name

_Thoughts & Messages
for the Happy Couple_

Guest Name

Thoughts & Messages
for the Happy Couple

Guest Name

_Thoughts & Messages
for the Happy Couple_

Guest Name

Thoughts & Messages
for the Happy Couple

Guest Name

Thoughts & Messages
for the Happy Couple

Guest Name

Thoughts & Messages
for the Happy Couple

Guest Name

Thoughts & Messages
for the Happy Couple

Guest Name

Thoughts & Messages
for the Happy Couple

Guest Name

*Thoughts & Messages
for the Happy Couple*

Guest Name

Thoughts & Messages
for the Happy Couple

Guest Name

*Thoughts & Messages
for the Happy Couple*

Guest Name

*Thoughts & Messages
for the Happy Couple*

Guest Name

_____

Thoughts & Messages
for the Happy Couple

Guest Name

_____

Thoughts & Messages
for the Happy Couple

Guest Name

Thoughts & Messages
for the Happy Couple

Guest Name

Thoughts & Messages
for the Happy Couple

Guest Name

Thoughts & Messages
for the Happy Couple

Guest Name

Thoughts & Messages
for the Happy Couple

Guest Name

Thoughts & Messages
for the Happy Couple

Guest Name

Thoughts & Messages
for the Happy Couple

Guest Name

Thoughts & Messages
for the Happy Couple

Guest Name

_____

Thoughts & Messages
for the Happy Couple

_____

_____

_____

_____

_____

Guest Name

_____

Thoughts & Messages
for the Happy Couple

Guest Name

Thoughts & Messages
for the Happy Couple

Guest Name

*Thoughts & Messages
for the Happy Couple*

Guest Name

Thoughts & Messages
for the Happy Couple

Gift Log

Gift	Received By

Gift Log

Gift	Received By

Gift Log

Gift	Received By

Gift Log

Gift	Received By

Thank you for your purchase! For more fun, unique guest books, log books, notebooks, journals and more, please take a look at www.amazon.com/author/booksbyjenna to view other wonderful books that you'll be sure to enjoy.

Printed in Great Britain
by Amazon